califia's daughter
poems

devorah major

Willow Books, a Division of Aquarius Press
Detroit, Michigan

califia's daughter

Copyright © 2020 by devorah major

All rights reserved. No part of this publication may be reproduced, stored in a retrieval system, or transmitted in any form, or by any means, electronic, mechanical, recording, photocopying or otherwise without the prior written permission of the publisher.

Editor: Randall Horton
Front cover art: "Califia" by Susan Shelton
Back cover art: "Mural of Queen Califia and Her Amazons," Mark Hopkins Hotel, San Francisco
Cover design: Aquarius Press

ISBN 978-1-7330898-9-0
LCCN 2020932078

"mixed ancestry" first appeared in *Deepest Valley Review*
"wind" first appeared in *black bleeds into green* Word Temple Press
"apricot" first appeared in *Essence Magazine*
"love me sultry" first appeared in *Verdinia Amour* Artichoke Press
"creation paradox" first appeared in *Patterson Literary Review # 26*
"earth memories" first appeared in *Cape Cod Poetry Review*

Willow Books, a Division of Aquarius Press
www.WillowLit.net

Printed in the United States of America

Queen Califia was a fictional African amazon whose name was used by Cortez to name California. Although I am thankful for and honed by my Bahamian family and ancestors, and although I acknowledge with great respect the other strands of my ancestry, California with its wild and open nature has shaped me to become who I am as woman, as elder and as poet. These poems are birthed from that experience as a daughter of this place. With its rocky cliffs and tossing waves. I am a daughter of Califia.

devorah major

Know ye that at the right hand of the Indies there is an island called California, very close to that part of the Terrestrial Paradise, which was inhabited by black women...They were robust of body with strong passionate hearts and great virtue. The island itself is one of the wildest in the world on account of the bold and craggy rocks.

From <u>The Adventures of Esplandián</u> (1510)
by Garcia Rodriguez de Montalvo

Table of Contents

califia's song / 7
black holes / 8
earth memories / 9
wind / 10
stardust / 11
almost drowning / 13
creation paradox / 15
afro-american song / 18
mixed ancestry / 19
on being an alien in outer space / 22
the shape of my body changes / 24
clouded musings / 26
my growing home / 27
daddy's girl / 28
chairs / 29
denim cut-offs / 30
returning home / 31
ode to james brown / 32
discipline / 34
my daughter / 36
for the record / 38
one morning / 40
dreaming poems / 42
aimless chatter / 43
world traveler / 44
missing words / 45
amends / 46
what are the consequences of silence? / 50

while my father rises / 51

closed mouth women / 53

last dance / 55

only in dreams / 57

cycles / 58

apricot / 62

love me sultry / 63

walking into love / 64

I choose love / 65

pillow talk / 66

seasoned love / 67

symphonic man / 69

waking without fear / 71

with arms open / 72

weighing in / 73

Note on Queen Califia / 74

califia's song

my heart does not sing songs
of hate, fear, or regret

for my name will be braided
into the lightening of time

califia, daughter
of seafaring mandinka

queen of amazon defenders
tamer of wild beasts

i have ridden the backs of griffins
to come to these rocks

where clothed in sea crystals
draped gold and the evening's wind

i savor freedom's harvest

black holes

black holes sing
in the key of B♭

hot and swirling

forming and
swallowing stars

as they breath
the universe in

earth memories

water
heat

color
everywhere

wings
fur
flesh

roots
gossamer and rope

seed   sea
loam and sand

an infinite ability
to birth
to heal
to kill
to die

the shape of wind
its sound

wind

motion
touch
change
sculpting life
around twig
mountain
nape sand wave
sometimes captured
always released

no death
no birth
just change

this planted
that flattened
another smoothed or sharpened

a cutting chill
a thick warm embrace

wind strokes

stardust

out of clay
they caution

dust to dust
they intone

from earth you came
and to earth you will return
they admonish

they remind us
we are mortal
and subject to death
yet insist on their eternals

demons and angels
paradise or purgatory

merely human
with a finite
measure of days

but we have
exploded as novas
burned through galaxies
explored far reaches of the milky way
ridden on the tails of comets
danced on the edge of asteroids
until

in a dizzying frenzy of passion

we fell

through the viscous ozone
past cooling clouds
to settle in the ooze
that feeds the ocean's floor

it was there that we decided
to grow limbs and tongue
all the while holding inside
the truth of our origin

magnesium
calcium
iron

we are the stuff
that stars are made of

it is a scientific fact
a cosmic trust

in ignorance
and in knowing
we hold grains of the divine
inside ourselves

and we always have

almost drowning

1.

in the midst of it all
i know i must come up
for air or quickly
learn to breathe
under water

2.

cresting ocean
above my head

i hold back the gasp
and open my mouth

deeply swallow air
in one huge gulp

before descending again
into the salted waters

to shoot up once more
towards the sun

unfold
absorb

lay back
inhale

before again
descending

3.

i dive
lower
than i can imagine

looking above i see
a glimmer reflecting
below the ocean's
choppy surface

i cut the waves
break through
for a moment

breathe
as i let the waves
return me to the shore

creation paradox

we hold the great-great
grandparents of our ancestors'
grandparents
in our bloodstreams
in our stomachs
in our hearts

thousands of years
rest inside our souls

in those years lives the record
of our beginning
it is the sweetest marrow in our spine
the cleanest shine in our eyes
the open side of our laughter

you can read it in the lines
on the soles of our feet

when we retell the stories
of where we came from
we draw back tree branches
to find hidden fruits which we savor
pointed thorns which make us bleed
the yesterdays that led to here
the here that leads to tomorrow

when we go back to the beginning
we find the stars

in the beginning
there was a time
we all say
when we were not

after that time we became

we were created

we were molded
we were spat out
we were sung into

until we learned
how to make
what to form
where to spit
why to sing

but once
long ago
in the beginning

there was only one
and from the one
others were born
and out of those many
came us

that is the story
we all tell

but
before that beginning
before the in the beginning
beginning when we were born

there must have been
another beginning

before the spider crafting web
laying sixteen eggs
before the mountain birthing lovers
birthing children
before the sky settling low
to mate with earth
before light
before darkness
before breath even

there must have been
another beginning

a beginning that lives
in a place we call
unknowable

yet is braided
into our genealogies

and it is said that
it is in this beginning
the beginning before our beginning

it is there that you must go
if you want to find
the faces of god

thousands of years
thousands and thousands of years
rest inside our souls

afro-american song

listen to the notes
sweet and hard
round and full
dark honied lava

jazz melodies
bebop riffs
blues grit

notes braided
with roots
growing deep
inside your soul
colored of ebony
and mahogany
sepia tones that will
break free

notes hearty and fierce
singing survival
singing endurance
singing time
all round the planet

humming with the stars
punctuating the seasons

round and full
honey and lava
sweet and hard
dark and long
jazz melodies
bebop riffs
blues grit
rocking
swinging
flying

mixed ancestry

i
a planet varied
sea to land
calm to storm
wondering in the mirror
where did the eyes come from
and the texture of hair
who contributed to the skin tones
and who to the lips
thoughtfully dividing the source
of my limbs
my hips
my face

i landless
homeless
being so much a mixture
a couscous of spices and fruits

a mongrel of the comings together
chosen and forced of so many different ones

a crossbreed that fills the spaces
between rich dark and translucent fair

a mutt that has unruly fur
cropping out in varied shades
ears and tail being strangely incongruent

a grafting of cultures
that insists where love fails
life will persist, thrive, recreate

a planet varied
mountains to hills
to valleys to chasms deep
waterfalls to rivers to streams
to oceans wide

a mélange i
claiming my space in the rainbow

on being an alien in outer space

> after Ruby Onyinyechi Amanze's "The Spaceship"

ancient alien theorists say
my blood reveals
my true origins-

that i began
in outer space

perhaps i came from those
who speak of ancient kin
who looked from african peaks
eons ago to a sky that held no moon
before the visitors' round ship arrived
and left their seeds among us

there are many clues to my origins

my feelings of almost always being an outsider
not quite fitting in anywhere
despite my excellent human-form camouflage

my resistance to the ideas of borders

my refusal from early childhood
to pledging allegiance to one small earth plot
when the universe is so inconceivably vast

my carrying a passport but
being without one true homeland

my missing the innate human impulse
towards war and domination

my fascination with stars
and my conviction that i am
a space traveler

all point to my existence as alien

i have in fact
circumnavigated the sun
more than sixty times during my life
always keeping about 93 million miles away
which still doesn't eliminate all sunburns

sun ra spoke often of being a venusian
so i am hardly the first or the only
alien

indeed this planet is full of aliens
but not all of us know it
or care to

the shape of my body changes

not long ago my body seemed formless
just a pulse and heat
all flesh consumed in passion
my spirit spread out
beyond the bones
through the blood
past the sweat
seeming to touch distant stars

less than a week before that
i had fins but no gills or tail
suddenly sleek as i pulled
through the tepid water
blue like the sky
cloudless and distant

sometimes my body is bloated
too full of waste
it bulges here and pinches there
cluttered with snot and trivialities

often it is round
able to go in many directions
at the same time
a constant circle of being

and then at times
my body is nothing
but a racing heart and
long elk legs darting
through a deserted glen

one morning last month
it was long and thin
at certain angles
hard to see
like the sudanese woman
belongings on her head
bright yellow and green caftan

swaying in the dry wind as she
draped with hunger
leads her children
through a war zone
to a war zone

my body shifts and changes
but always caresses the air
enjoys the breath of stilled wind
against breast or thigh
through hair

my body remains
a simply cast temple
of love and forgiveness

clouded musings

"Whisper your dream to a cloud. Ask the cloud to remember it." Yoko Ono

clouds are heavy with tears and dirt
hovering above smog particulates
briefly carrying seagull feathers
dressed in colors they do not choose
moving only as the wind demands
weighing as much as 100 elephants

let the clouds feed the jade tree
which blossoms in gratitude from those kisses
let the clouds shelter the squabbling blue jays
from the swelter of summer heat and melting tar
let the clouds dress the mountain tops
in undulating cloths of white and gray
now a hat, then a cloak

let the clouds stay as clouds
while my dreams fly
always returning to settle
in a crevice of my open heart

my growing home

open breaths
jazz jam laughter
family as salve and thorn
blankets cradling
in winter frosts
fragrant spices wafting

the safety
to be wrong or awkward
silly and sublime

a chorale of freedom

daddy's girl

always been a daddy's girl
just because of the way
he liked to watch me grow
stronger or brighter
or even crazier

thought i could
expand forever
yet still be safe in his
long strong daddy arms

as words seduced me
tortured and amused me
made me their tool and toy
never thought through
this string we share
this legacy of syllables

my mother chanted peace
as my father demanded struggle
and i learned how to spell rebel
and rebel under his watch

the trees i climbed
the kites i flew
the dances i spun
the words i crafted
grew from his boisterous laugh
scary discipline
watchful dominion

if i am woman true
it is because i've grown
as daughter of a father
who showed me
how to swing
and when to duck
and why to never stop reaching
for the redolent spirals of freedom

chairs
after Lonnie Holly him and her hold the root

grandpa's chair didn't rock
it reclined, back tipped
feet out, a leathered throne
for the towering cinnamon man

we were only allowed to sit
in grandpa's chair
when he wasn't home
or when he was in the backyard
weeding his vegetable plots
tending his apple trees
or sitting in the shade
in front of the shed
sipping the minty ice tea
that grandma and i made

but we had to move
out of the chair
before his face peeked
through the living room door

one day i was too slow
i jumped up
with a mumbled "sorry"
mixing little girl smile with real concern

surprised when he chuckled
and gently told me to sit back down
as he settled across from me
in grandma's matching chair
and soft-voiced began to weave
me a story as i perched
on the edge of his chair

grandpa's love was
a deep underground river
that showed itself in unexpected ways
the water always sweet and fresh

denim cut-offs

after Annie Mae Young's *"Bars" Work-clothes quilt*

we patched our jeans
muted blue squares
hidden on the inside
so that only
the torn lines at the knees remained

hinting at the skinned knees
from bike skids
or roller skate splats
or two-left-feet falling
over themselves races
that caused the tears

then when the pants hems
were too tattered
and patches too small
to repair the wear
we cut the legs off
about mid-thigh
and folded the raw edges
up and under
designing cuffed shorts

only now do i think
of the quilts that
we could have crafted
from the sheared
pants bottoms
we carelessly stuffed
into the trash

returning home

1.

a boy in khaki shorts and sandals,
loped down the packed dirt road
black skin sweating years of sun kisses
a large package balanced on his head

as we rode to aunt margaret's new providence house
with her avocado trees weighted with ripe fruit

africa i queried my father, who drove the tree-lined narrow street
bahamas he answered, *but yes in many ways the same, home*

2.

eleuthera rocky and green, dressed in smooth white and pink beaches
adorned with empty conch shells humming deeply, home

the ancestors accepted this long thin island as their home
despite hurricane whirl and growl, our family was planted

and we grew thick and lush, spreading branches
bearing fruit under her skirts until she gently urged us out

ode to james brown

james brown you could
take the growl, take the howl
turn it, twist it pump it

shake the drums, push the horns
fire up the cymbals and make hot african winds
blow across the waters, climb the mountainsides

you could reach up into the heavens, good lord
and storm back down again
to make us scream with you
grunt and groan and sweat
baby, baby, baby,
baby, baby, baby

we heard you james brown
roll your gospel heart into r&b

you would exhale your wails
layer your squalls and grunts
weave your tales of
love and sweat, power and revelation
into a poly-rhythmic prism of fire and funk

until we'd be the ones pleading
please, please, please
as you came back strong
did another turn, split to the floor
jumped back up and screamed out
for the drummer to come along
cause you had the feeling
and you were the song

all the while our hips never stopped turning
and our feet kept sliding across the floor
while you made us sweat, made us do like you said
and give the drummer some- one
give the drummer some- one, two
give the drummer some- one, two, three, four

and take a measure for ourselves

we were busy polishing the floor
when you'd snatch it back up
do a split turn and, scream out for more

cause you could make us spell
hard and work fifty different ways
shining brown and gold, flashing red capes
calling it *a man's world*
then crumbling to the floor

while we women smiled knowing
it was always more than that

polished obsidian soul
was you james brown
hard, rich, slick, thick
deep, hurtin', loving
was you james brown

feeling good, so good
and making us feel good too
cause when *papa got a brand new bag*
we got new kicks, knees and elbows
flapping funky 'cause you were *super bad*

you spit the gospel soul funky truth
into the earth of every continent
touched souls on either side of two centuries-
great- grands through babies still raising fists
singing it loud to remind each other
we black and we proud.

so me, when i think on you, james brown
all i can do is try and *get on the good foot.*
say all i can do when i turn
my mind and heart to you, james brown
is think, *think, think, think about the good* things.

discipline

discipline was simple once

defined by strict rules
and jerking alarms
punching mornings
into textbooks, sharp pencils
and lined paper

in time discipline
transformed
metronome precision
to iron pole back
pulled in hips
feet pointed hard
until the arch cried
thigh lifted up
until it cramped
and quivered

but then one night

when coltrane and i
ate the dawn together
spinning circles
as we stretched the walls of my apartment
beyond the trembling trolley lines
above the heaving fog

discipline became

a strong but cruel lover
who helped me find
the ecstasy of my dreams
as companion and tormentor
touchstone and shackles

years have passed
and we rest easy now

discipline does not beat
or confine me
it is my road map and ladder
the key in which
i sing my songs

it is myself
in and outside of
the wild of me

my daughter
for yroko

my daughter
is plums in may
juice not yet sweet
flesh thick and soft

my daughter
is hips that swing across street corners
and a mouth that pouts and curls
in between plaints

the hair never right
the pimple that will come
the clothes that aren't in
the dance she hasn't learnt
the teacher who doesn't see
and the mother who always wants more
and will not settle for less

my daughter
makes our days a battle ground
finds nos in a valley of yeses

her room is a hurricane
her tongue tempts the gutter
her spirit flies with angels
her smiles soothe the aged

she is breath
i am eyes
she holds my heart
we build her dreams

my daughter reminds me
of the splendor of the explosion
vibrant, loud, electric

as i sing to her
of the grandeur of the hum
resonating, sustained

for the record

>   for my son Iwa and the executed Shaka Sankofa and his brethren

'An eye for an eye, and we'd all be blind.' Gandhi

i watch my son move into manhood
the music video slant in last year's step
translated to a wider stride that intones
his name/man of good character

he saunters with more than sinews and bone
my son makes his own air when the
oxygen is in short supply

my son is blood of purpose
heart of resolve
lips of laughter
he calculates, computes, splits ideas
delineates, assesses, adds and subtracts
recombines the moments of his days
and moves forward

my son has never been beaten until his brain scabbed
or been trapped in a childhood of bruising injustice

my son was not produced inside frosted crack pipes
seeking a mother constantly disappearing in wisps of acrid smoke

he was not chased into closets under beds down dark alleys
by large fisted, black booted men disguised as fathers
or uncles or friends

i watch my son unwrap his future
like a child at a first birthday party
tearing apart the colorful paper
getting caught up in the string
not knowing what to play with first

yet the brighter his glow
the more i see the other boys

these children still
who would be men
who pace in chains and shaved heads
around a future that makes bowels liquid
bladders weak and faces contort
as they add stars to the tattered flag
that shines on this nation's affliction
their arms tied down and
filled with vengeance's poison

my son sings his song each night
i listen to the notes that hold inside the
cries of these boys who would have been men
if given a road, if offered a dream

one morning

i sit in a kitchen
where pies have cooled
on every available surface save
the linoleum tiled floor

i sit in a kitchen where
rice steamed; biscuits browned
stews simmered and chickens roasted

where tempers raged
and passions boiled up and over
the formica counters

i sit sipping sweet milky coffee
while watching a hummingbird
suck nectar from a lemon blossom
on the tree i planted

as i push loneliness to the corner
of a seldom opened drawer
place it underneath the long wooden spoons

dreaming poems

i spent the night dreaming poems
waking with no time to catch them

they grew from a heavy sleep
pulling me into a club
where i was on a stage
rhymes gliding
sliding through under
astride my fingertips
as i stepped out

raging across the stage
finding a beat inside a beat
for those elongated minutes
a dancing riffing black storm

later as morning began to yawn
clear pictures
that held answers and music
between the lines
inside the meter
around the center
flowed towards dawn

but when i awoke
only the flavor remained
all substance was left
in sleep

aimless chatter

words collide
coil around themselves

they turn their backs on me
indifferent to my call

they collude to stop my poems
lay low in the dry soil

hide all their colors

world traveler

translated and blurred
we trade languages

land, tongue, touch
bridges quickly built

slurred across syntax
their meaning vague

we think we share
our thoughts perhaps it

is only smiles shrugs nods
words we speak fail

missing words

my words split

they tore themselves apart
letter by letter

vowel sounds hum intermittently
constants whine and clang
silent letters meditate on nothingness
and there is no sense between them

my tongue is scalded unable
to touch the back of my teeth
to flatten for diphthongs
or curl up to touch palate

i am waiting for the words to return
to let me again find the nouns
connect with the subjunctives
seduce the adjectives
and dance with the verbs

amends

have i told you that i love words

that i embrace them as my constant lover
am always available early dawns
rain filled evenings and midnight moonrises
or when sun burns her way
through the midday fog

paying heed to their insistent call
melting like warm honey
when they put their fire
to my fingers
to my tongue

have i told you that i love words

then i have lied
for i love them true
but not all the time

sometimes it is only a silly flirtation
a distraction from fast food television
something to do when the floorboards creaked
and night's thickness made me tremble
a hermit's plaything
an isolate's reason
a litany chanted in a room of fun-house mirrors
a ritual of form
complete with holy water and incense

i have spit words out
as so much phlegm
laced with strands of blood

i have squandered words in gutters

washed them down sewers
treated them as waste
to be buried or burnt

i have shredded words
until they became scraps
crowding the corners of my room

i have turned my back and ignored them
called them shallow and flat
declared that only music
could speak to me
and then refused to listen

i have sat with nursery rhymes
circling my skull
and made praise of doggerel

i have taken words for granted
scraped them like mud on the
mat i use to wipe my feet

i have shown words my disrespect
left them like flavorless gum
on the bottom of my desk

it is not the words' fault
they have only done
what i have asked

if they cowered in corners
it is because i beat them
if they winced and then splintered
at awkward angles

it is because i screeched
denied them their truths
and muffled their rhythms

if they hid until
they became faint with hunger

it is because i called them whore
became a pimp and secured tricks
in high-rise buildings
with elevators that went only
from basement to roof and back
to basement again

i have betrayed words

it was not love
but obsession
the need to control
to manage
and have dominion
over chaos
it was habit and addiction
it was greed

so they abandoned me
just got up and walked
like a cuckolded spouse
cleaned out the house
took all the furniture
cut off the phone
and left no note

i begged them to come back
sent them scented notes
lit candles to reveal a road back
prayed and fasted
admitted all my sins

until they returned
calling the shots

making me climb
from beneath thick downy comforter
to be chilled in the morning's night

lifting me out of a steaming bath
to leave puddles of bubbles

and the scent of jasmine
as a trail across the floor

again i pull my car to the shoulder of the road
write notes on the bottoms of tissue boxes
ink phrases on newspaper margins

the words are laughing at me

but they stay now
as long as i treat them kindly
as long as i love them truly

and i do love them

have i told you i need words
that they are my cornbread and greens
my summer melons and winter yams

though i have been unfaithful
again i love them true

what are the consequences of silence?

i search for silence inside myself
hear at times the rush of blood

my heart's cadence
punctuated with an extra gasp

at night
with no music or blinking screen
blinds open to the sky
starred here, more than city
less than desert or mountain

walking barefoot on the lawn
my feet folding grass blades
evening settling darkly
solar lights blinking on one at a time
my breath sounds

as car tires whoosh
doors shut
refrigerator hums
and my thoughts are
a cacophony of gibberish

in the darkest part of morning
my husband's breath next to me
the turning and shudder of sheets
a whisper
a psalms

silence, as in to not speak?

what of the inner noise or music
chants or chatter
that fill my ears

i do not know silence's consequences
because i do not know its truths

while my father rises

cat-lives long gone
my father rises
yet again

his doctors suspect
that he may be
more than human

stand in awe of his resilience
no longer provide calendars
pointing to a probable death date

but written words
have become
hieroglyphics

and friends, like dreams,
slip away leaving only
a memory of sweetness

still he makes me laugh

as he regales me with stories

chops that one last
chicken thigh for a coconut curry

while together
we mix his caribbean
spice mélange

but I have seen him
cry and tremble
at each new darkness

that is not the sheen
and sharpness of obsidian
but instead a thick icy fog

that causes streets to disappear
and veils mountains from the sun

closed mouth women

closed mouth women
do not speak of feasts and celebrations
do not remember the smokiness of saffron
cinnamon's sweetness
pungent garlic
or biting cayenne

fresh baked bread
does not haunt them

and sugary melon juice
of autumn afternoons
is long forgotten

they choose not to eat
as a way to drive out their sadness
as a penitence for being human and flawed
as an atonement for sins no one can recount

their skin is draped across their bones
like pale shirts carelessly hung on wire hangers
translucent fabric displaying blue-veined threads
crossing islands of embroidered purples and reds

closed mouth women fade
like the feeling of hunger
when perhaps they take
a few swallows of sweetened dark coffee
or nibbles of chocolate melting on the tongue
or fingertips of barbecue sauce
that remind them of laughing grandchildren
and sweat-washed summer evenings

always just a bite
or two to please
their insistent kin

closed mouth women share

a slow and secret dying

as they reveal an appetite
only for hunger
and carefully ladled love

last dance
> for my mother

angular and just to the side of the beat
hips hitting the four corners
with joy and determination
if not much grace

you loved to dance

every photo of you dancing
is full of the glow of your smile
and the rock of your head
as the music tossed you
to and fro

so when you began your
dance with death
you were comfortable in its rhythms
even refused food so you could get
that much closer

wrap your boney limbs around
death's dry skeleton frame
the two of you softly slow jamming
around the room

finally when too weak to stand
you took to your bed
and watched death dance around you
as you lifted your hands
in its rhythmed patterns

your lips and toes were painted
siren red, your fingernails too
filed and glossed

your nightgown cotton, flowers and lace
as clean as it was loose and you
ready to go to the ball

we saw you resting in between songs
to offer a brief *I love you*
to a granddaughter, a great grandson,
your new son-in-law, me
and then losing interest
your eyes would glaze over
you would throw off
the comforter and sheet
ready for the next dance

until that october morning's sunrise
when you found a lasting shelter
in death's icy arms
swaying softly
let's go
       let's go
              let's go
until the music stopped
and the last dance ended

only in dreams

      for my father

only in dreams
your voice the silence of a dark cave
your skin walnut brown wrinkled around smiling eyes

your voice the silence of a dark cave
who you are/were is the lesson of stars, distant galaxies
the jar of spices- paprika, rubbed sage, garlic granules needs replenishing

who you are/were is the lesson of stars, distant galaxies
i am caught up in tears odd moments, feeling absence as chasm
knowing my shape twisted and sublime is a constant reflection of you

i am caught up in tears odd moments, feeling absence as chasm
yet you still bring me the orange of nasturtiums, the sweetness of plum
it's like when i was a child and everything was forever new

you still bring me the orange of nasturtiums, the sweetness of plum
your skin walnut brown wrinkled around smiling eyes
only in dreams

cycles

in this season
this harsh
uncompromising
season

in this season

which will be one
of the two thousand
seasons through which
we sift the grains
of our experience

as we learn how to make
a better now

as we learn why to maintain
a more compassionate how

in this gray though radiant time
there is so much loss

a freedom
a liberty
a confidence in the inevitability
of love or the unwavering
surety that there are
more kind people
in the world than cruel
more people full of caring
than bitter with apathy

that there is more resolve than fear
more possibility than tragedy

and then there are
the inevitable deaths

the losses of those

whose absences
create spaces
that seem to be bordered
only by the edges of eternity

spaces that we try to embroider over
with memories and photographs
anecdotes and tears

creating a silken filigree
that can be torn apart
by the softest breeze

until we are left again
with the deep bowl of sadness
that makes up so much
of these days
these times

in this season

when we are shown that
our lives have become
unending lessons
on receiving golden gifts
that we must
inevitably let go of

over and over again we must
receive and let go
receive and let go
receive and let go
with blessings
and with grace

what are our lives
but pushing
and climbing through

understanding that
who and what we love

who and what we lost
has not in truth
been wrenched from our arms
or quietly slipped away

has not disintegrated
or been destroyed

but has instead been transformed
into another purpose
into another form

what is this journey as human
but passage through and over
infinite crossroads
which offer up
pain and celebration
as our wings beat against
and finally break through
the tight cocoon of life

and what is life
but loss and gain
inside the music
of our breath

and what must we learn
but to forgive
and to surrender
but to love
and to let go

but to place no more and no less weight
on our tears than on our laughter

apricot

a ripe apricot hangs
just beyond my reach

it is an easy climb
past a sturdy trunk
to where it swings

blushed gold, fragrant
tempting me
to capture its perfume
on the tip of my tongue

my fingers flutter
with the leaves
as i pull myself upwards
steadied by a lower branch

it rocks in the wind
threatens to fall
if i move too slowly

love me sultry

love me sultry, deep night blue
moonbeams for covers, starlight and you.
love me in colors that welcome the dawn
moroccan rose perfumes wrapped in your arms.

give me no grayness, sour and tired
limping fog mornings, mud stiff and mired.

love me in purples, oranges and gold
like juicy ripe melons, flesh sweet and bold.
green scented laughter, brown shadowed touch
love me in colors that tell me so much.

i'm done with crying and missing the dawn
waiting for lovers, who've long come and gone.
love's tinted palette, you've shown me its charms
drenched me in its honey, all fragrant and warm.

love me lushly, deep night blue
moonbeams for covers, starlight and you.

walking into love

with eyes
wide open

skies a clear
expanse of blue

i step forward
into love's seams

i choose love

not seeking perfection
nor the puzzle

piece falling
perfectly into place

broad strokes
unexpected turns

i unlock the
doors of my heart

and choose love

pillow talk

i like the way you talk to me
your words flow through me
your consonants make me tremble
your vowels make me sigh

i like the way you talk to me
the roll of your g's
the softness of d's
hard and deep
long and gentle
thoughtful thrusts
punctuated with silences
and questions
pauses and insistence

i like the way you talk to me

touching my insides
listening for my response

seasoned love

i
love heat's many shades

as a preteen i stood
above a blasting heating vent
hot air drying, even more
my rash laden legs
but soothingly warm
as i leaned over
the huge speaker cabinet
my father built years before

i sang with dinah
as if i understood what
she meant when she said
she *covered the waterfront*
and was *watching the sea*

vowed that when i met my him
i would ask him to *teach me
teach me tonight*

years later winter rain wet
i would race home
fill the fireplace
light it up
and let otis make me
warmer as he sang of sitting
near the dock of the bay
fog horns moaning

as he watched the boats and whistled
and i stretched my bare toes
closer to the sparks

when grown i made a habit
of lying on my bed
set low beneath undraped windows
a crack of blue sky seen as

i yielded my birth scarred belly
my thick-thighed, curly haired self
to the caressing fingers of the sun's heat

so what could i do
when you opened your fiery heart to me
and asked me to enter

when you wrapped your strong
and gentle arms around me
and began to stroke the sweat out of my pores
until it rolled slowly down around
my breasts past your lavish lips

what could i do
when you held winter at bay and
let me lie in the heat of your embrace
that could make hot sweet bubbling syrup
from rock salt

what could i do but
love you back

symphonic man
for Gregg

don't want me no one note man
think he so fine that all
he got to do is turn and flash some
pearly whites and all the gals
just waiting to spread they legs

'cause when the glow wears off all you got
is stale conversation and dried sweat
for me he just a one note man
playing a worn-out tune

don't need me no one verse man
say he got some money in his pocket
and ain't afraid to spend
buy a this and shop for a that but

don't open nothing
not a door or a mind or a heart
oh you can ooh and ah about the car he drive

but one tired trite verse is all I hear

don't have time for no one song guy
full of manners for sure can pull a chair out
carry a package but ain't got clue the first
on listenin' to what a woman has to say or think
how she feel about herself, or the world

he be just a one hit jingle, tinny and thin

see I have no desire for a one hit wonder

'cause I got me a masterpiece of a man

with a body of music that stretch
from one century to the next

he got an opus of skills

honed by years of living and reaching
tuning and retuning
he a man who can handle
all the instruments of love

i be singing love in sonorous duets
since i found me my philharmonic man
who give me everything i need

and best of all he don't make that music
for nobody but me, every day and every night
he offers me up a lush and sumptuous
love story symphony

ain't nobody else need to even wave a hand
cause i got me a forever symphonic man

waking without fear

there was sun
there was laughter
touching and sweat

there was an album to be bought
after searching through used record store bins

there was forgiveness
there was safety
there was trust

love had a shape
its name was ours

with arms open

i embrace you love
though i have at times
hidden from your touch
because i thought you smothered me
required that i be the air
for others to breathe
the water for others to drink

i embrace you love
though i have at times
denied your advances
knowing that for me to accept your gifts
i must offer those of my own

i embrace you love
having known you
as ladder and crutch
when i wanted to dance,
to walk, to sit in stillness

i embrace the dreams you send me
and the tears that spill in moments
when you crack open my heart
to remind me how full it is
of star shine and silk

i embrace you love
who will not catch me when i fall
but instead advise me to swim
in your surging waters

i embrace you love
though you know no forgetting
and insist i continue to feed
on your fruit of forever

ever more powerful
you make me claim you
as intimate companion

weighing in

my life is a scale
tipped to yes
yes to family
yes to community
yes to the heavens
yes to the earth
yes to pleasures of flesh and spirit
yes to life and all its attendant
chores and obligations
yes to struggle
yes to love

Note on Califia:

The state of California was named after Queen Califia. It is said that Africans came across sea currents to arrive in South America and then moved east and west through Mexico and around the gulf settling in the south, mixing blood and dance, color and culture with the people of the corn. Cortez's crew of six hundred held two hundred Africans who worked its sails, cleaned its decks and sometimes served as interpreters. Because of this, Cortez thought that Africans populated this part of the world too. He named this land California, the isle of Queen Califia.

But where did he get the name? It is believed by some that the legend of Califia was initially formed by seafaring Kalifuna Mandinka who arrived in the new world before Columbus. African Moors who traded and sailed with their Mandinka brethren brought the tale of Calfia to Spain where, around 1510, (pulp) novelist Garcia Rodríguez de Montalvo in Las Sergas de Esplandian (The Adventures of Esplandian) refashioned the tale of a compassionate, fearless, and beautiful African Amazon queen living on a steep, rocky-cliff, gold-rich island. With Queen Califia were fierce and able female subjects, hundreds of griffins, wild beasts harnessed in gold, and occasional visiting (or captured) men. Some also assert that California once held a vast inland lake, and appeared to be an island for hundreds of years, and that during this time it was explored by a few of these early Kalifuna Mandika voyagers, and that it is, in fact, the actual land of the Califia myth.

Acknowledgments

This book is very family centered and so my thanks must start with family. My family, particularly my grandparents, parents, children and husband have inspired many of these poems. My Bahamian kin and ancestral land inspired others. My daughter Yroko helped immeasurably in the actual shaping of this book. Poet sisters Opal Palmer Adisa and giovanni singleton gave me insights which strengthened several of the poems. I must also acknowledge the San Francisco African American Historical and Cultural Society who gave me free run over their library which led to my first discovery of Queen Califia. Thank you to Aquarius Press and Randall Horton as editor of their Willow Books imprint for being open to such a wide palette of voices. I am honored to be one the threads in their tapestry.

www.ingramcontent.com/pod-product-compliance
Lightning Source LLC
Chambersburg PA
CBHW021131080526
44587CB00012B/1235